Carl STAMITZ

(1745 – 1801)

Concerto No. 3 for Clarinet in Bb and Orchestra
B flat Major / Si bémol majeur / B-Dur

Piano Reduction by
Gero Stöver

DOWANI International

Preface

Carl Stamitz was one of the leading violinists and composers of his day. Although he produced a large body of orchestral and chamber music, he is especially valued for his instrumental concertos, particularly those for the clarinet, which had only recently been invented. Our revised new edition with solo part and piano reduction introduces you to his Concerto No. 3 in B flat Major for clarinet and orchestra. The piano reduction was prepared by the pianist and arranger Gero Stöver.

The CD opens with the concert version of each movement. After tuning your instrument (Track 1), your musical work can begin. First, you will hear the piano accompaniment at slow and medium tempo for practice purposes. At slow tempo you can also hear the clarinet played softly in the background as a guide. Having mastered these levels, you can now play the piece with orchestra at the original tempo. Each movement has been sensibly divided into subsections for practice purposes. You can select the subsection you want using the track numbers indicated in the solo part. The full cadenzas are only played in the concert version. Each practice tempo gives you time to play a very brief cadenza; you can find the entrance after the cadenza with the aid of metronome clicks. Further explanations can be found at the end of this volume along with the names of the musicians involved in the recording. More detailed information can be found in the Internet at www.dowani.com. All of the versions were recorded live.

We wish you lots of fun playing from our *DOWANI 3 Tempi Play Along* editions and hope that your musicality and diligence will enable you to play the concert version as soon as possible. Our goal is to give you the essential conditions you need for effective practicing through motivation, enjoyment and fun.

Your DOWANI Team

Avant-propos

Carl Stamitz fut un violoniste et compositeur remarquable de son époque. Il composa de nombreuses œuvres orchestrales et de la musique de chambre. Ses concertos sont également d'une grande importance, en particulier les concertos pour clarinette – un instrument encore relativement jeune en ce temps-là. Cette édition révisée avec une nouvelle partition, comprenant réduction pour piano et partie soliste, vous présente le concerto n° 3 pour clarinette et orchestre en Si bémol majeur de Carl Stamitz. La réduction pour piano a été réalisée par le pianiste et arrangeur Gero Stöver.

Le CD vous permettra d'entendre d'abord la version de concert de chaque mouvement. Après avoir accordé votre instrument (plage n° 1), vous pourrez commencer le travail musical. Pour travailler le morceau au tempo lent et au tempo moyen, vous entendrez l'accompagnement de piano. Au tempo lent, la clarinette restera cependant toujours audible très doucement à l'arrière-plan. Vous pourrez ensuite jouer le tempo original avec accompagnement d'orchestre. De plus, chaque mouvement a été judicieusement divisé en plusieurs passages à travailler. Vous pouvez sélectionner ces passages à l'aide des numéros de plages indiqués dans la partie du soliste. Les cadences entières ont été enregistrées seulement dans la version de concert. Aux tempos de travail vous aurez le temps de jouer une très brève cadence ; le métronome vous aidera à trouver l'attaque après la cadence. Pour obtenir plus d'informations et les noms des artistes qui ont participé aux enregistrements, veuillez consulter la dernière page de cette édition ou notre site Internet : www.dowani.com. Toutes les versions ont été enregistrées en direct.

Nous vous souhaitons beaucoup de plaisir à faire de la musique avec la collection *DOWANI 3 Tempi Play Along* et nous espérons que votre musicalité et votre application vous amèneront aussi rapidement que possible à la version de concert. Notre but est de vous offrir les bases nécessaires pour un travail efficace par la motivation et le plaisir.

Les Éditions DOWANI

Vorwort

Carl Stamitz war ein bedeutender Violinist und Komponist seiner Zeit. Er komponierte zahlreiche Orchester- und Kammermusikwerke. Eine große Bedeutung haben jedoch auch seine Konzertkompositionen, vor allem die Konzerte für Klarinette – ein damals noch recht junges Instrument. In der vorliegenden revidierten Neuausgabe mit Klavierauszug und Solostimme präsentieren wir Ihnen das Konzert Nr. 3 für Klarinette und Orchester in B-Dur von Carl Stamitz. Der Klavierauszug wurde von dem Pianisten und Arrangeur Gero Stöver erstellt.

Auf der CD können Sie zuerst die Konzertversion eines jeden Satzes anhören. Nach dem Stimmen Ihres Instrumentes (Track 1) kann die musikalische Arbeit beginnen. Zum Üben folgt nun im langsamen und mittleren Tempo die Klavierbegleitung, wobei im langsamen Tempo die Klarinette als Orientierung leise im Hintergrund zu hören ist. Anschließend können Sie sich im Originaltempo vom Orchester begleiten lassen. Jeder Satz wurde in sinnvolle Übe-Abschnitte unterteilt. Diese können Sie mit Hilfe der in der Solostimme angegebenen Track-Nummern auswählen. Die Kadenzen werden nur in der Konzertversion komplett gespielt. Bei den Übe-Tempi haben Sie jeweils Zeit für eine sehr kurze Kadenz; den Einsatz nach der Kadenz finden Sie mit Hilfe von Metronomklicks. Weitere Erklärungen hierzu sowie die Namen der Künstler finden Sie auf der letzten Seite dieser Ausgabe; ausführlichere Informationen können Sie im Internet unter www.dowani.com nachlesen. Alle eingespielten Versionen wurden live aufgenommen.

Wir wünschen Ihnen viel Spaß beim Musizieren mit unseren DOWANI 3 Tempi Play Along-Ausgaben und hoffen, dass Ihre Musikalität und Ihr Fleiß Sie möglichst bald bis zur Konzertversion führen werden. Unser Ziel ist es, Ihnen durch Motivation, Freude und Spaß die notwendigen Voraussetzungen für effektives Üben zu schaffen.

Ihr DOWANI Team

Concerto No. 3

for Clarinet and Orchestra
B flat Major / Si bémol majeur / B-Dur

C. Stamitz (1745 – 1801)
Piano Reduction: G. Stöver

DOW 7501

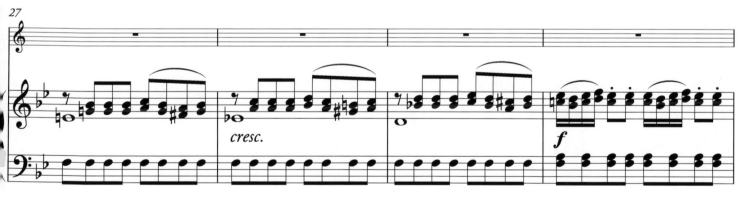

6

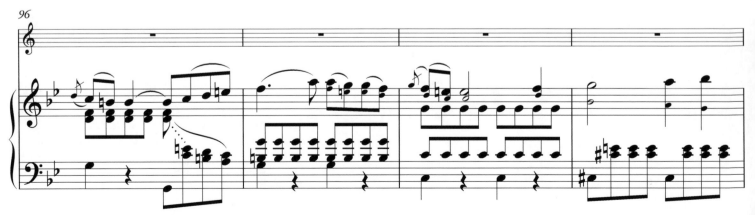

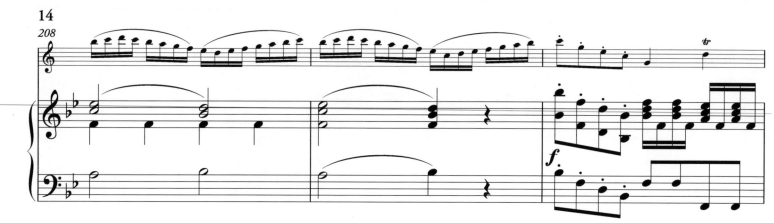

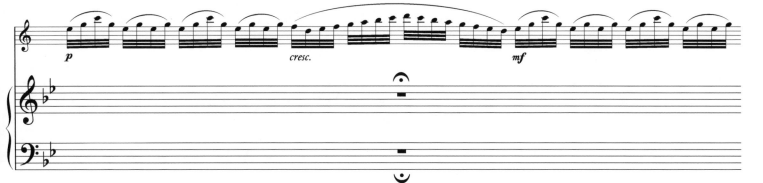

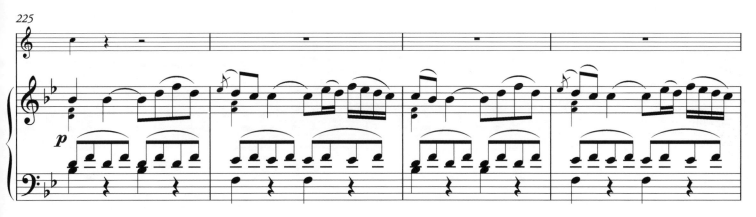

16

Rondo

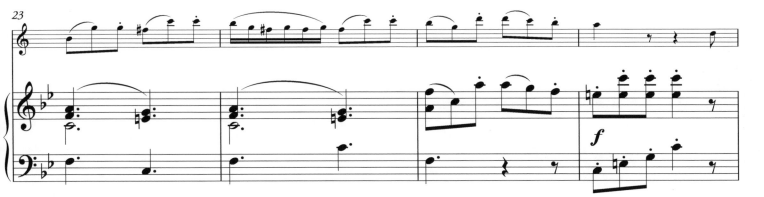

(Eingang)

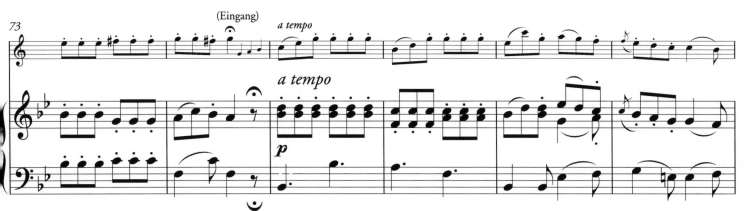

Cadenza

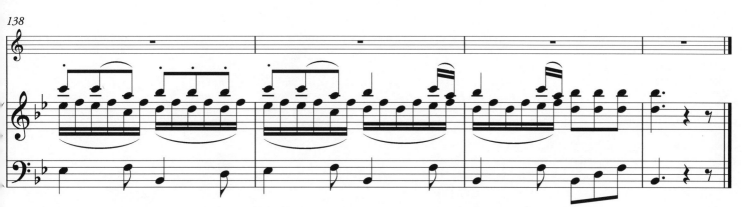

ENGLISH

DOWANI CD:

- Track No. 1   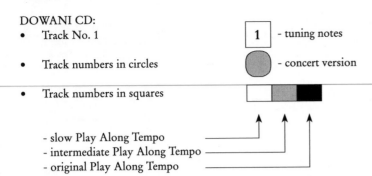   - tuning notes

- Track numbers in circles   - concert version

- Track numbers in squares

    - slow Play Along Tempo
    - intermediate Play Along Tempo
    - original Play Along Tempo

- Additional tracks for longer movements or pieces
- **Concert version:** clarinet and orchestra
- **Slow tempo:** piano accompaniment with clarinet in the background
- **Intermediate tempo:** piano accompaniment only
- **Original tempo:** orchestra only

Please note that the recorded version of the piano accompaniment may differ slightly from the sheet music. This is due to the spontaneous character of live music making and the artistic freedom of the musicians. The original sheet music for the solo part is, of course, not affected.

Cadenzas: The full cadenzas are only played in the concert version.

FRANÇAIS

DOWANI CD :

- Plage N° 1   - diapason

- N° de plage dans un cercle   - version de concert

- N° de plage dans un rectangle

    - tempo lent play along
    - tempo moyen play along
    - tempo original play along

- Plages supplémentaires pour mouvements ou morceaux longs
- **Version de concert :** clarinette et orchestre
- **Tempo lent :** accompagnement de piano avec clarinette en fond sonore
- **Tempo moyen :** seulement l'accompagnement de piano
- **Tempo original :** seulement l'accompagnement d'orchestre

L'enregistrement de l'accompagnement de piano peut présenter quelques différences mineures par rapport au texte de la partition. Ceci est du à la liberté artistique des musiciens et résulte d'un jeu spontané et vivant, mais n'affecte, bien entendu, d'aucune manière la partie soliste.

Cadences : Les cadences entières ont été enregistrées seulement dans la version de concert.

DEUTSCH

DOWANI CD:

- Track Nr. 1   - Stimmtöne

- Trackangabe im Kreis   - Konzertversion

- Trackangabe im Rechteck

    - langsames Play Along Tempo
    - mittleres Play Along Tempo
    - originales Play Along Tempo

- Zusätzliche Tracks bei längeren Sätzen oder Stücken
- **Konzertversion:** Klarinette und Orchester
- **Langsames Tempo:** Klavierbegleitung mit Klarinette im Hintergrund
- **Mittleres Tempo:** nur Klavierbegleitung
- **Originaltempo:** nur Orchester

Die Klavierbegleitung auf der CD-Aufnahme kann gegenüber dem Notentext kleine Abweichungen aufweisen. Dies geht in der Regel auf die künstlerische Freiheit der Musiker und auf spontanes, lebendiges Musizieren zurück. Die Solostimme bleibt davon selbstverständlich unangetastet.

Kadenzen: Die Kadenzen sind nur in der Konzertversion komplett eingespielt.

DOWANI - 3 Tempi Play Along is published by:
DOWANI International
A division of De Haske (International) AG
Postfach 60, CH-6332 Hagendorn
Switzerland
Phone: +41-(0)41-785 82 50 / Fax: +41-(0)41-785 82 58
Email: info@dowani.com
www.dowani.com

Recording & Digital Mastering: Pavel Lavrenenkov, Russia
CD-Production: MediaMotion, The Netherlands
Music Notation: Notensatz Thomas Metzinger, Germany
Design: Andreas Haselwanter, Austria

Concert Version
Gerhard Kraßnitzer, Clarinet
Austrian Symphony Orchestra Burgenland
Boris Perrenoud, Conductor

3 Tempi Accompaniment
Slow
Nora Dancsik, Piano

Intermediate
Nora Dancsik, Piano

Original
Austrian Symphony Orchestra Burgenland
Boris Perrenoud, Conductor